KEY TO
FOURTH YEAR LATIN

(Revised Edition)

BY

ROBERT J. HENLE, S.J.

LOYOLA PRESS.
Chicago

FOREWORD

The present key for *Fourth Year Latin* does not contain translations of the selections from Virgil, of those from Sacred Scripture, or of those from Christian writers, of all of which so many good translations are immediately available that no purpose would be served in giving others here.

In the translation of the *Pro Archia* parentheses are frequently used to bring out the meaning more clearly in English or to supply what the author omitted but what is easily understood from the context. Occasionally variant meanings and more exact expressions are thus indicated.

In the exercises the author has endeavored to use only words that are to be found in the vocabulary and in *Pro Archia*. Where others appear they are merely a guide to the teacher, and give the more exact idiom. It is not desirable to have the ordinary student use this more exact expression for the time being, as the vocabulary that he must master is already sufficiently ample.

Teachers can readily recognize the correctness of student translations that are at variance with the key, yet based on the vocabulary. For that reason the translations do not pretend to exhaust all the possibilities. Thus there are a number of words in English which have more than one Latin equivalent. "I kill," for example, has six, any one of which might be correct. Alternates such as *te* and *vos, laudas* and *laudatis,* are not indicated.

Where an explanation of the underlined construction is desired in the exercises it would be well for the teacher to demand fuller explanations than those given in the key. Only that much is given in the key which is considered essential for a correct explanation. By such complete answers the students will familiarize themselves with the grammatical construction as well as the example that is intended as a key to the understanding of the rule.

THE DEFENSE OF ARCHIAS

Address to the Jury

Delivered by

Marcus Tullius Cicero

1. If there be any natural talent in me, gentlemen of the jury, and I am aware of how slight it is, or if I have any skill in oratory, in which I do not deny that I have had some little practice, or if I possess any knowledge of the theory of this art of my profession, gleaned from the pursuit and training of the liberal arts—to which, I confess, I have never at any time of my life felt any disinclination—my client Aulus Licinius should rightly be the very first to claim the benefit of all these gifts of mine.

For as far back as my mind can look over the past, and recall the earliest memories of my boyhood—going back even that far—I see that he has been my inspiration both in undertaking and in pursuing my course of studies. Now, if this voice of mine, trained by his exhortation and precepts, has been on occasion a source of safety to some persons, then surely I ought, as far as I can, to lend aid and protection to the man from whom I have received that gift which has made it possible for me to assist others and even save the lives of some.

But to avoid anyone perhaps thinking it strange that I speak in this way, on the plea that my client is possessed of a different kind of talent, and has not scientific training in oratory—I myself have never devoted myself exclusively to this one field. For all the arts which have to do with culture have a certain common bond, and are linked together by a certain interrelationship.

2. However, so that it may not seem strange to any of you that, in a legal inquiry and in a state court, when a case is being pleaded before a praetor of the Roman people, a most upright man, and a stern body of jurors, and in the presence of such a crowded assembly, I should employ a style of speech which is at variance not only with court traditions but even with forensic language, I ask you, in this present case, to grant me a permission—most suited to our defendant, and, as I hope, not disagreeable to you—namely, that when I am pleading the case of this great and learned poet, in the presence of this cultured group of men, men of your refinement and lastly, before our praetor presiding at this trial, you will allow me to dwell rather

1

freely on the pursuit of culture and literature, and, in the cause of such a character, who because of his quiet and studious life has had little or no experience in court trials, to make use of a new and rather unusual type of speech.

And if I feel that you allow and grant me this permission, I shall certainly cause you to think that my client should not only not be removed from the lists of citizenship, since he is a citizen, but that even if he were not a citizen, should have been admitted to citizenship.

3. For as soon as Archias emerged from boyhood and (outgrew) the studies in which boys are ordinarily trained to refinement, he devoted himself to the work of writing, first at Antioch—for it was there that he was born of noble family—a city once populous and prosperous, the home of many learned men and of liberal studies, rapidly outstripping all his fellows in the renown of his talents.

Later on, in other parts of Asia Minor and everywhere in Greece, his arrival was attended with such throngs that the desire of seeing him surpassed the rumor of his genius, while the welcome given him on his arrival and the admiration he aroused surpassed even these high expectations. In Italy at the time Grecian arts and sciences were very much in vogue; and these studies were at that time more popular in Latium than they are now in the same cities, and here too at Rome, because of the peaceful state of the country, they were not disregarded.

As a result of this, my client was presented with citizenship and other awards by the people of Tarentum, Locri, Regium, and Naples, while all who had any right to pass judgment upon true genius deemed him worthy of their acquaintance and hospitality. When he had become known to those whom he had not yet met, by such widespread reputation, he came to Rome during the consulate of Marius and Catulus. From the first he found consuls of whom one could supply him with great achievements about which to write, while the other could furnish not only achievements, but also give interested attention (to his writings).

At once the Luculli received him into their home, although at the time Archias was still attired as a boy. It was a proof not only of his literary genius, but also of his character and good qualities, that the family which was the first to show him favor as a youth was also dearest and most intimate to him in his old age. In those days, Q. Metellus, the hero of the Numidian war, and his son Pius took a liking to him; M. Aemilius used to listen to his poetry; he found ready welcome at the home of both the Quintus Catuluses, father and son; and L. Crassus sought his friendship. Moreover, since he was bound by ties of close friendship to the Luculli, Drusus, the Octavii, Cato, and the entire Hortensius family, he was treated with the highest honor, in that he was courted not only by those who were eager to learn and hear (his poems), but even by such as made a pretense perhaps of learning and hearing (them).

4. Meanwhile, after a rather long interval had elapsed, during which he had gone with M. Lucullus to Sicily, and was leaving that province with the same Lucullus, he came to Heraclea. Since this was a city enjoying full treaty rights (with Rome), he desired to be admitted to citizenship in it, and obtained his wish from the Heracleans, both because he was considered worthy on his own account, yet especially because of the influence and favor of Lucullus. By the law of Silvanus and Carbo (Roman) citizenship is granted (in the following terms): Whoever shall have been enrolled in a federated city, provided that they have a residence in Italy at the time the law was passed, and provided that they report to the praetor within sixty days. Since my client had already made his residence in Rome for many years, he reported to his dear friend, Q. Metellus.

If we are speaking of nothing but the law of citizenship, I say nothing more; the case is finished. For which of these points, Gratius, can be disproved? Do you deny that he was enrolled at Heraclea at the time I speak of (*tum*)? There is a man present of the highest authority, most conscientious and trustworthy, M. Lucullus, who states that he does not merely think it is true, but knows it; who says he not merely heard it, but saw it, not only took part in it, but did it. We have with us representatives from Heraclea, upright men, who have come on account of this trial with documents and official affidavits, men who affirm that my client was enrolled as a Heraclean.

Do you demand here the public records of the Heracleans, which we all know were destroyed during the war in Italy, when the record office was burned? It is absurd to disregard the evidence that we have and demand evidence that we cannot obtain—to pass over in silence the living memory of men and appeal to the memory of records. It is absurd, when you have the conscientious word (*religio*) of a most eminent man and the sworn oath of a most incorruptible city, to reject evidence that cannot possibly be tampered with, while you demand records, which you yourself admit are wont to be falsified.

Or (would you say that) my client had no residence in Rome, in spite of the fact that for so many years, before he was granted citizenship, he made Rome the center of all his goods and fortunes?

5. Or did he not report? He did indeed report according to those records which (are) the only ones from that registration list and that board of praetors (that) possess the authority of public records. For, although the records of Appius were said to have been kept rather carelessly, and Gabinius' lack of responsibility (fickleness), as long as he was unaccused (safe), and the deprivation of civic rights after his conviction had destroyed all confidence in his records (of the records), Metellus, the most conscientious and discreet man of (them) all, was so careful (was with such diligence) that he came to Lucius Lentulus the praetor and to the jury, and said that he was disturbed because of the erasure of a single name. On these records, therefore, you see no erasure on the name of Aulus Licinius.

This being the case (since these things are so), why is it that you doubt about his citizenship, especially since he has been enrolled also in other cities? For, at a time when men in southern Italy (*in Graecia*) were freely granting citizenship to many unimportant persons, and to those endowed with some little or no artistic ability (skill), I suppose the Regians or the Locrians or the Neapolitans or the Tarentines refused to give to this man, endowed with ability of the highest renown (with the highest renown of native ability), what they were accustomed to grant to stage artists! Moreover, when others, not only after citizenship had been granted (after the grant of citizenship), but even after the *Lex Papia* (had been passed), crept somehow or other onto the records of their municipalities, will this man be rejected who does not even make use of those (records) in which he is enrolled, because he always wanted to be a Heraclean?

You demand our census lists. Of course! For it is a secret that at the time of the last censors this man was accompanying (with) that most illustrious general, Lucius Lucullus, with the army; that at the time of the preceding censors, he was with the same man, (who was then) quaestor in Asia; that when the first censors were in office, Julius and Crassus, none of the people were enrolled (no part of the people was listed). But, because the census list does not establish the right of citizenship and only indicates that he who is enrolled so conducted himself already then at that time as (for) a citizen, he, whom you are accusing of having enjoyed even in his own judgment no rights of Roman citizens, has often made a will according to our laws, and has received (entered upon) the inheritances of Roman citizens, and has been reported among (those recommended for) rewards to the treasury by the proconsul Lucius Lucullus.

6. Seek proofs, if you can (find) any. For never will he be convicted either in his own judgment or in the judgment of his friends.

You will ask us, Gratius, why we are so greatly pleased with this man. (It is) because he furnishes us (a place) where both our mind may be refreshed after (from) this noise of the forum and our ears (when) worn out by wrangling may have rest. Or do you think that material for speaking (what we speak) on such a variety of subjects could hold out for us, unless we cultivate our minds with learning, or that our minds could endure such a strain, unless we refresh them with the same learning?

I admit, of course, that I have devoted myself to these pursuits. Let others be ashamed, if they have so buried themselves in books that they can neither contribute (bring) anything from them to the common good, nor bring anything to light for humanity (bring anything forth into the light and sight). But why should I be ashamed, who have lived for so many years, gentlemen of the jury, in such a manner that never has my leisure drawn me away from anyone in need of help (from the need or assistance of no one), never has pleasure called me away, nor finally has sleep delayed me (when any one was in need of help). Who, therefore, would rebuke me, or who would be justly angry at me, if I shall have taken as much time for renewing these studies as is allowed to others for transacting their business, for celebrating the holidays at the games (celebrating the festive days of games), for other pleasures or even for the rest of body and mind, or as much time as others give to protracted banquets, or finally to gambling or playing ball?

Moreover, this ought to be allowed me the more (readily), because from these pursuits my (this) oratorical ability (speaking and ability) is also developed, which, however trifling it is in me, has never failed my friends in danger (has never failed the dangers of friends).

If this ability seems of little account (rather slight) to anyone, at all events (indeed) I know from what source I may draw those principles (things) which are certainly of the greatest moment. For, unless I had persuaded myself from youth by the precepts of many persons and by much reading that nothing in life is greatly to be sought after except merit and uprightness, and that, while pursuing it, all tortures of mind and body, all dangers of death and banishment are to be considered of slight importance, never would I have exposed myself (thrown myself into) for your safety to so many and such great struggles and to the daily attacks of unprincipled men. But all literature (books), the sayings of wise men, and history are filled with examples, which would all lie in darkness, unless the light of literature were added to them. How many pictures of the most courageous men the Greek and Latin writers have portrayed and left for us (have left portrayed), not only to be contemplated, but even to be imitated! Holding these always before me in administering the state, I was molding my mind and heart by the very thinking of remarkable men.

7. Someone will ask: What? Those illustrious men themselves, whose virtues have been handed down by literature, have they been educated in that learning which you extol with your praises? It is difficult to state this with certainty about all (of them); but, nevertheless, what I answer is certain. I admit that there have been many men of remarkable character and manliness without learning, and by an almost godlike disposition of nature itself have stood forth by themselves as self-controlled and serious-minded men. This also I add, that more often has nature without learning led to (had power towards) praise and virtue than learning without nature. Moreover, this likewise I contend, that when to an exceptional and distinguished nature there shall have been added a certain systematic training in learning (a certain method and training of learning), then there usually (is accustomed to) exists a certain remarkable and unique result (something or other).

From this number is this man whom our fathers have seen, a godlike man, Africanus. From this number is Gaius Laelius, Lucius Furius, very self-controlled and temperate men. From this number a most courageous and at that time a most learned man, that (grand) old man, Marcus Cato. These men certainly would never have devoted (betaken) themselves to the pursuit of literature (those things), if they were not helped by literature to the acquisition and cultivation of virtue.

But if this great benefit were not apparent (were not shown), and if pleasure alone were sought from these pursuits, nevertheless, as I think, you would judge this to be a most refined and broadening relaxation of the mind. For other relaxations are not suited to every occasion or to every age or to every place (are neither of all times nor of all ages nor of all places). But these pursuits nourish our youth, bring delight to old age (delight old age), enhance prosperity. They afford a refuge and solace in adversity. They bring enjoyment at home, do not hinder (it) abroad. They pass the night with us, go abroad, and sojourn with us in the country.

But if we ourselves are able neither to attain these things, nor to appreciate them (taste them with our senses), nevertheless we ought to admire them, even when we see (them) in others. 8. Who of us was so boorish (of such churlish spirit) and unfeeling (hard) that he was not affected recently by the death of Roscius? This man (who) though he died as an old man, yet on account of his outstanding skill and charm seemed altogether not to have deserved to die. Therefore he won for himself the love of all of us by the mere movement of his body; shall we (then) neglect the incredible movements of the mind and the quickness of genius?

How often I have seen this (man) Archias, gentlemen of the jury— for I am imposing on (I use) your kindness, since you are attending so closely to me in this new method of pleading—how often have I seen this man, when he had written not a single word, speak extempore a great number of excellent verses about things which were then being carried on, and how often when encored (recalled to repeat them) (have I seen him) speak the same thing, changing the words and sentences! And (when) he wrote them down with care and thought, I have seen them so approved that they approached the praise (that is given to) of ancient writers. And shall I not love this man, shall I not admire him, and shall I not consider that he is to be defended in every possible way?

And so we have received (this doctrine) from the greatest and most learned men, that the pursuit of other things depends (*constare*) on teaching, rules, and theory, (but) a poet has power from nature herself, and is stirred up by the powers of the mind and is inspired by a certain almost divine breath. Wherefore in his own right our famous Ennius calls poets "holy," because they seem to be recommended to us by some gift and present as it were of the gods.

Let therefore, gentlemen of the jury, the name of poet be inviolable among you, the most cultured (of) men, (a name) which no uncivilized nation has ever desecrated. Rocks and solitudes reply to the voice (of poetry), often savage beasts are turned aside by song and stand still; and we trained in the best things, shall we not be moved by the voice of poets? The Colophonians say that Homer is their fellow citizen, the Chians claim him as theirs, the people of Salamis recollect he is theirs, the people of Smyrna have established him as their citizen and accordingly have dedicated a shrine to him in their town; very many other peoples besides fight among themselves and contend (he is their fellow citizen).

9. Therefore those people seek for (claim) a stranger, because he was a poet, even after his death; and shall we reject this living man, who is ours both by his own preference (will) and our laws, especially since hereafter Archias will bring all his zeal and all his genius toward glorifying the glory and praise of the Roman people?

For as a youth he touched upon Cimbrian affairs and he was agreeable to that famous Gaius Marius, who seemed somewhat unimpressionable (*durior*) so far as these pursuits are concerned. For no one is so estranged from the Muses that he will not easily allow the eternal eulogy of his labors to be committed to poetry. They say that the famous Themistocles, the greatest man at Athens, said, when it was inquired of him, what actor or whose voice he most willingly listened to: "(the voice) of him, by whom his own valor was best proclaimed." Also the famous Marius in like manner in a special way loved Lucius Plotius, by whose talent he thought that the things he had done could be made famous.

And indeed the Mithridatic war, a great and difficult (war) and waged in a great variety of circumstances both by land and sea, all of this was related by this man; which books make famous not only Lucius Lucullus, a very brave and most famous man, but they also make the name of the Roman people famous. For the Roman people, under the command of Lucullus, opened up the Pontus, fortified by one time kingly resources and by nature herself and the place (in which it is located); the army of the Roman people, under the same leader, with a not too large band of men, put to rout innumerable forces of the Armenians; it is in praise of the Roman people that according to the counsel of this same man, the most friendly city of the Cyziceni was snatched from every regal attack and from the mouth and jaws of a total war and preserved; our incredible and famous (*illa*) naval battle at Tenedos will always be brought forward and praised, when with Lucullus fighting and the leaders killed, the fleet of the enemy was sunk; ours are the trophies, ours are the memorials, ours are the triumphs.

By whose genius these things (*quae*—which things just listed above) are brought forward, by the same geniuses is the fame of the Roman people glorified. Dear to Africanus the elder was our Ennius, accordingly also it is thought that he is set up in marble on the tomb of the Scipios; and by those praises certainly not only he who is praised but also the name of the Roman people is enhanced. The great-grandfather of this man, Cato, is praised (raised) to the skies; (and) great honor is added to the affairs (exploits) of the Roman people. Finally all those famous Maximi, Marcelli, Fulvii cannot be praised without at the same time honoring all of us (cannot be honored without the common praise of all of us).

10. Therefore our ancestors received as a citizen (into citizenship) that famous man who had done these things, the man of Rudiae; and shall we eject from our city this Heraclean, (who is) sought for (claimed) by many cities, and is established (as a citizen) in this one by our laws?

For, if anyone thinks that a smaller mead of glory (less profit of glory) is to be had from Greek poetry than from Latin, he grossly errs, for the reason that Greek is read in almost all nations, whereas Latin is confined within its boundaries, (and) truly narrow ones (at that). Wherefore, if the things we have done are bounded by the regions of this earth, we should desire that whither the javelins of our armies have come, thither should our glory and fame penetrate, for since these things are honorable to those people about whose affairs works are written (*scribitur*), then certainly this will be a very great inducement (to undergo the difficulty) of dangers and labors for those certainly who fight at the risk of life for the sake of glory.

How many chroniclers of his exploits is the famous Alexander said to have had with him! And indeed when he stood at the tomb of Achilles in Sigeum, exclaimed: "O fortunate youth, who has found a Homer as the herald of your valor!" And rightly. For, unless the famous Iliad had arisen, the same tomb which hides his body, would also have blotted out his name.

What? Did not our great Pompey, who balanced fortune with valor, (equalled fortune with valor), present Theophanes of Mytilene, the chronicler of his affairs, with citizenship, in a mass-meeting of soldiers, and those great brave men of ours, nothing but rustics and soldiers, they approved the act with a great shout, excited by a certain sweetness of glory and participants as it were in the praise of this one man? Accordingly, I suppose, that if Archias were not a Roman citizen by law, he could not have brought it about that he should be presented with citizenship by some commander or other! For Sulla, when he was (accustomed to) giving citizenship to Spaniards and Gauls, would, I suppose, have refused it to this man when he requested it; we have seen this man (Sulla) in a mass-meeting. when a mediocre poet from among the people thrust up to him a book, which made epigrams concerning him, with only every other verse a little longer, at once order that a reward be given him from among the things which he was then selling, but with this condition, that he write nothing in the future. He, who thought that the industry of a mediocre poet was worthy none the less of some reward, would he not have sought out the talent of this man, his ability in writing and his fluency (*copiam*)? What? And from Quintus Metellus Pius, his most intimate friend, who presented many with citizenship, would he not have sought citizenship either through himself or through the Luculli? This man (Quintus Metellus Pius) who most of all so desired (verses) to be written concerning his exploits, that he gave his attention (ears) even to poets born at Cordova, (whose poetry) sounded (agrees with *poetis*) rather dull and provincial (foreign).

11. And this fact which cannot be hidden, we must not conceal from ourselves, but keep before our eyes: we are all led by a desire for praise, and the greatest men especially are inspired by fame. Great philosophers inscribe their names even in those books which they write on the contempt of fame. In the very (book) in which they despise publicity and honor, they wish their names (*nominari*) to be publicized.

Indeed, Decimus Brutus, a great man and a general, adorned the entrances of temples and the monuments of his kinfolk with the poems of Accius, a great friend of his. Further, that Fulvius who fought with the Aetolians in company with Ennius, did not hesitate to consecrate the spoils of Mars to the Muses. Therefore, in that city in which generals fresh from the field honored the name of poet and the temples of the Muses, judges in civil attire should not shrink from the honor of the Muses and the safety of poets.

That you may do all this the more willingly, I will indict myself before you, and confess to my own love of glory, a love too eager perhaps, but still upright. For the things I did together with you in my consulship for the safety of the city and the empire and for the life of the citizens and for the whole state, these things my client has touched upon and begun in his verses. When I heard of this, since the undertaking seemed to me important and pleasant, I urged him to complete it.

No other reward does virtue desire for its labors and perils than that of praise and fame; if this reward be taken from us, what reason would we have for exercising ourselves in heavy labors in this narrow and brief span of life? Indeed, if the soul looked forward to nothing in the future, and confined all its thoughts to the same limits by which the space of life is enclosed, it would not break itself in such weary labors, nor be distressed by so many cares and watchfulness, nor so often fight for life itself. But now there dwells in every good man a force which night and day stirs the soul with incentives of glory and warns it that the remembrance of our name will not cease with the time of life, but is to be compared with all future generations.

12. Should all of us who are engaged in the service of the state and in these perils and labors of life seem to be so small of soul that, though to the end of our days we have drawn no calm and peaceful breath, we should think that all things will die together with us? Many great men eagerly have left behind statues and images, not representations of their souls but of their bodies; should we not much rather wish to leave behind a likeness of our counsels and virtues wrought and finished by great geniuses? I indeed, even in the very act of achievement, considered that I was scattering and sowing all the things I achieved for an eternal remembrance over the whole earth. Whether this remembrance will be absent from my consciousness after death, or, as the wisest of men have thought, will pertain to some part of my soul, I am at the present time certainly delighted with the thought and hope thereof.

For these reasons, gentlemen of the jury, preserve a man of such character as you see approved both by the worth of his friends and also by the duration of their friendship, of such talent as can appropriately be estimated from this that you see him sought out by the genius of the greatest men, with a case proved by benefit (support) of the law, the authority of the city, the testimony of Lucullus, the records of Metellus. Since this is the case, we ask of you, gentlemen of the jury, if there ought to be any, I do not say (*modo*) human but even divine recommendation in the case of such talents, to take under your protection a man who has always done honor to you, your generals, the achievements of the Roman people, who promises to give an eternal testimony to our and your recent domestic perils, and who belongs to that number of men who always by all men have been considered and called inviolable, so that he may rather seem to have been relieved by your humanity than outraged by your severity.

What I have said briefly and simply about the case, in accord with my custom, gentlemen of the jury, I trust has been approved by all;

the things I have said about the defendant's talent and in general about studies themselves, which are foreign to the custom of the forum, and the usage of the court, these I trust have been taken in good part by you, gentlemen of the jury; I am quite certain that they have been thus taken by him who gives the decision.

EXERCISES BASED ON CICERO

LESSON 1

Exercise 1.—retardārit—retardāverit; resignāsset—resignāvisset; repudiāsset—repudiāvisset; exīstimārunt—exīstimāvērunt; dōnārunt—dōnāvērunt; conciliārat—conciliāverat; āvocārit—āvocāverit; interīsse—interiisse; audīsse—audīvisse.

Exercise 2.—1. As far as in us lies . . . (To the best of our ability . . .). 2. All the arts which bear upon culture . . . (All that goes to make up culture . . .). 3. It has at times been the salvation of some people . . . (To some it sometimes proved a boon . . .).

Exercise 3.—1. Quārē, jūdicēs, laudandus est Archiās. 2. Haec ratiō dīcendī in Archiā nōn est. 3. Quoad mēns Cicerōnis spatium praeteritī temporis respicit, Archiās eī prīnceps ad ingrediendam ratiōnem hōrum studiōrum exsistit. 4. Archiae et ingenium et ratiō omnibus nōbīs est laudanda (sunt laudanda). 5. Quārē pueritiae (nostrae) memoriam recordēmur ultimam. 6. Quantum est situm in nōbīs Archiae opem ferre dēbēmus. 7. Aulum Licinium cīvem esse Rōmānum ostendam. 8. Archiās vir erat summā hūmānitāte. (Archiās vir summae hūmānitātis erat). 9. Quārē hōrum studiōrum ratiōnem profectō ingredī dēbēmus (Quārē ratiō hōrum studiōrum nōbīs profectō ingredienda est). 10. Summum in eō ingenium erat et disciplīna (exercitātiō dīcendī). 11. Eratne in Cicerōne ingenium exiguum? 12. In exercitātiōne dīcendī mediocriter versātus est, nec ūllum aetātis ējus tempus studiīs optimārum artium ac disciplīnā abhorruit. 13. Profectō Archiās in prīmīs frūctum ā Cicerōnis disciplīnā repetere dēbet.

LESSON 2

Exercise 4.—1. Rōma artibus et disciplīnīs (līberālissimīs studiīs) tum adfluēbat. 2. Hīc Rōmae Lūcullus eum domum suam recēpit. 3. Nōmen Rōmānum (populī Rōmānī) celebrāvit. 4. Prīmum (in) Lūcullī domum receptus est. 5. Fīlius ējus ad Asiam profectūrus est. 6. Summa Rōmae erat exspectātiō. 7. Ā puerō amīcus Lūcullī erat (Lūcullō ā puerō amīcus erat). 8. Hōc nōn est forēnse genus dīcendī (Haec dīcendī ratiō ā forēnsī sermōne abhorret). 9. Hīc propter ōtium et studium quaestiōnēs lēgitimās ignōrābat (ā quaestionibus lēgitimīs aliēnus erat). 10. Haec studia omnium sunt aetātum.

13

Exercise 5.—1. Before men of your refinement (culture) . . . (In the presence of so cultured an audience . . .). 2. I shall certainly succeed in convincing you of this (see to it that you come to this conclusion). 3. Thanks to (Because of) his quiet life of study. . . . 4. He took up writing (He devoted himself to a literary career). 5. He was highly honored (held in the highest esteem). 6. Lest it appear surprising to any of you . . . (That none of you may think it strange . . .).

Exercise 6.—Models: A. If I have (am possessed of) any ability . . . (If there is any natural ability in me . . .). B. Lest anyone marvel at (this) . . . (Let no one be surprised . . . for . . .).

1. Num quis mīrētur mē eum dēfendere cui tantum dēbeō? 2. Sī quid est in mē virtūtis (Sī ūlla in mē est fortitūdō) eum dēfendere dēbeō. 3. Cicerō, nē cui mīrum vidērētur, cūr Archiam dēfenderet exposuit (ostendit). 4. Sī quae (qua) causa est, dīc (eam) nōbīs. 5. Interrogāvit num quī mīlitēs adessent (Interrogāvit adessentne aliquī mīlitēs).

Exercise 7.—Models: A. The noblest men are spurred on by fame (The better a man is, the more he is influenced by fame). B. He marks each one of us for slaughter. C. The one gave him (furnished him with) exploits (to write about), the other gave him his attention (appreciation).

1. Optimus quisque litterārum studiō dēditus est (litterīs studet). 2. Optimus quisque ad virtūtem colendam semper sē cōnfert (semper virtūtem colit). 3. Caesar ūnumquemque laudāvit, quod fortiter pugnāvisset. 4. Ex hīs duōbus (Hōrum duōrum (virōrum)), alter ad artem dīcendī, alter ad scrībendī studium sē contulit. 5. Suam quisque mortem timuit (timēbat).

Exercise 8.—Models: A. Some one or other said this. B. There are those who fear him (Gr. 634). C. He had been for some years (now) at Rome. D. He has a certain other ability.

1. Est quaedam in optimō quōque virtūs quae (eum) ad glōriam cōnsequendam agitat (concitat) (quā ad glōriam cōnsequendam dūcitur). 2. Sunt quī litterīs dēditī nōn sint (nōn studeant). 3. Audīvī nesciōquem hoc dīcentem (dīcere). 4. Quaeret quispiam (aliquis), "numquid glōriae est in studiō litterārum?" 5. Jam aliquot annōs studiō dīcendī dēditus es.

Exercise 9.—Models: A. No one at all believes this (And there is no one who believes this). B. He said he could give a way (method) to absolutely no one.

1. Ecquis (Num quis) est quī nesciat Archiam fuisse clārum (prae-

clārissimum) poētam? 2. Negāvit quemquam esse quī sē nōn esset laudātūrus, quod Archiam dēfendisset (Negāvit esse quemquam quīn sē laudātūrus esset, quod Archiam dēfenderet (i. e., *at the time*)). 3. Rogāvit num quis negāret (negātūrus esset)[1] Archiam esse cīvem Rōmānum. 4. Negāvit sē eīs quidquam esse datūrum. 5. Negāvit sē ūllī Gallō fidem habitūrum esse.

Exercise 10.—Ōrātiō quā Cicerō Archiam, summum poētam atque ērudītissimum hominem sibique familiārissimum, dēfendit ūnō ferē annō post mortem Catīlinae est habita. Quō tempore Cicerō ab omnibus ferē Rōmānīs colēbātur et ab eīs ipsīs, quī inimīcī ējus fuerant, summō honōre afficiēbātur. Neque tum (id temporis) Rōmae erat quisquam quī aptior esset (magis idōneus esset) ad hanc causam dīcendam, in quō nōn tantum esset summa auctōritās, summa cōpia et virtūs dīcendī, summumque ingenium—quod, quamquam ipse dīxit esse exiguum, scīmus (tamen) fuisse maximum—sed etiam ipsī optimārum artium studiō, cui Archiās semper operam dabat, aliquot jam annōs dēditus erat (sed etiam ad ipsum optimārum artium studium, cui Archiās semper dēditus erat, sē ante plūrēs annōs jam contulerat). Sī quis (quisquam) Rōmae poētam et hominem ērudītum dēfendere dēbuit, Cicerō certē dēbuit.

Exercise 11.—Amīcitiam optimus quisque semper laudāvit, de quā ipse Cicerō librum (libellum) (cōn)scrīpsit, in quō eam nōn sōlum magnōpere laudat, sed etiam quam ūtilis sit ostendit (dēmōnstrat, expōnit). Amīcī enim est, ut opīnor, amīcum quantum potest (quantum in sē est) adjuvāre, ā perīculīs dēfendere, servāre ab impetū inimīcōrum. Neque quisquam negābit aliās (quoque) esse causās, cūr amīcitiam laudāre dēbeāmus (amīcitia sit laudanda). Nam etsī (quamquam) sunt quī simulent sē amīcitiam contemnere, quod sēsē ipsī velint tuērī et dēfendere, tamen omnēs hominēs, quōdam ipsīus nātūrae habitū, amōrem cēterōrum (aliōrum) dēsīderant (cupiunt), ut etiam iī, quī ab aliīs auxilium (opem) quaerere nōlunt, amōris cupiditāte ad amīcos conciliandōs (parandōs, sibi jungendōs) dūcantur. Cum itaque illī (alterī) auxilium ab amīcīs, hī (alterī) sōlum amōrem quaerant, omnēs (tamen), ut dīxī, eō saltem ad amīcitiam laudandam dūcuntur, quod amīcos ipsī habent (colunt).

Exercise 12.—Quoad longissimē potest mēns mea respicere spatium praeteritī temporis, mātrem meam videō omnibus et temporibus et

---

[1] *Negāret* translates the direct "Num quis neget?"; *negātūrus esset* translates the direct "Num quis negābit?"

locīs (semper et ubīque) mē prae cēterīs (in prīmīs) amāvisse. Neque quisquam negābit ējusdem hortātū praeceptīsque hanc mentem esse cōnfōrmātam. Nam puerum (mē) ad virtūtem colendam, ad omnibus serviendum, ad Deum amandum semper (nunquam nōn) hortābātur. Num quis (ecquis) igitur mīrētur mē laudāre mātrem (quod mātrem laudō)? Nam sī quid in mē est virtūtis, sī quis optimārum rērum amor, sī quae (qua) probitās, haec omnia potissimum mātrī dēbeō.

LESSON 3

Exercise 13.—1. He could not speak for fear (Gr. 784, 982). 2. Because all came to light in the Senate, I shall explain it to you. (Gr. 572). 3. Due to his love of glory he devoted himself to a literary career (Gr. 992). 4. Since this is the case, do not doubt about his citizenship (Gr. 578). 5. Metellus was praised by Cicero for having kept the records with such care (Gr. 576). 6. Cicero praised Archias because he composed verses on the spur of the moment (Gr. 576). 7. They found fault with him for having formed a conspiracy (Gr. 576). 8. Rejoicing at this victory, he went to Rome (Gr. 782). 9. I rejoice because of his victory over the enemy (Gr. 576). 10. Because of the capture of Sicily, they were unable to buy grain (Gr. 913). 11. Fortunate he to have had Cicero defend him (Gr. 627). 12. These ships returned to port because they were unable to hold their course (Gr. 572). 13. Since this is the case, leave the city (Gr. 578). 14. The Gauls were blamed for making war without a cause (Gr. 576). 15. He praised Cato for having devoted himself to the study of literature (Gr. 576).

Exercise 14.—1. Archiās ab Hēracliēnsibus cīvitātem impetrāvit, quia (quod) eum dignum (cīvitāte) putābant (existimābant, dūcēbant). 2. Summō honōre afficiēbātur, quia (quod) Lūcullōrum (Lūcullīs) amīcus (familiāris) erat. 3. Cīvitātem impetrāvit, quia domicilium in Italiā diū habēbat. 4. Cicerō eum laudāvit, quod poēta et erudītus esset. 5. Cīvitātem impetrāvit quia domicilium Rōmae habuerat (habuisset) et Hēracleae adscrīptus (erat) et apud praetōrem professus erat (esset). 6. Lēgātī Hēraclea vēnerant, quod (quia) Lūcullī (id) volēbant (voluērunt). 7. Cicerō negāvit sē posse tabulās pūblicās prōferre, quod corruptae essent. 8. Cum habeāmus amplissimī virī religiōnem, pūblicās flāgitāre (poscere, requīrere) tabulās profectō (certē) rīdiculum est. 9. Gaudeō Cicerōnem dēfendisse Archiam (Gaudeō quod Cicerō dēfendit (dēfenderit) Archiam), quia (quod) Archiās (hic) dignus erat cīvitāte. 10. Optimus quisque poētās admīrātur, quod praestantissimō ingeniō (summā ingeniī glōriā) sint praeditī. 11. Nunc (Jam) sē vīcisse gaudent (Hāc victōriā gaudent). 12. Tabulāriō incēnsō, Cicerō tabulās pūblicās prōferre nōn potuit. 13. Prae timōre loquī nōn poterant (potuērunt). 14. Archiās in cīvitātem ascrīptus est. 15. Cicerō Archiam laudāvit, quia ipse litterīs dēlectābātur (propter suum (ipsīus) litterārum amōrem). 16. Litterās numquam parvī dūxī (aestimāvī). Ex hīs enim crēscit haec ōrātiō et facultās (dīcendī facultās), quā amīcōs dēfendere potuī. 17. Cicerō rem pūblicam dēfenderat maximē quia exīstimābat nihil nisi laudem atque honestātem esse magnōpere expetendum (quod nihil nisi laudem atque honestātem exīstimāret magnōpere esse expetendum. The subjunctive *exīstimāret* is not strictly logical here, but it is correct idiom). 18. Cum causa dicta sit (causā dictā), domōs¹ redeāmus. 19. Archiās ex Siciliā profectus est, quia Lūcullus, amīcus ējus, Rōmam īre voluit. 20. Prae gaudiō loquī nōn potuit. 21. Cum dē lēge dīxerimus (Quoniam dē lēge dīximus), causa dicta est. 22. Cicerō laudāvit Archiam, quod pollicitus esset, aeternum sē tēstimōnium laudis populī Rōmānī nōminī datūrum esse. 23. Prae tempestāte venīre nōn poterat (potuit).

Exercise 15.—1. Caesar explōrātōrēs praemīsit, quod hostēs collem tenērent (occupāvissent). 2. Rē pūblicā ē perīculīs ēreptā, grātiās Deō agere dēbēmus. 3. Explōrātōrēs captī sunt, quod (quia) mīlitēs nōn vīderant. 4. Propter timōrem in silvam fūgit. 5. Caesarem veritus (Propter metum Caesaris; Quod Caesarem metuēbat), in silvam fūgit. 6. Dux reprehēnsus est, quod sermōnem nōn scrīpsisset. 7. Cum jam sit nox (Quoniam jam nox est), domum redeāmus. 8. Mīlitibus fortiter pugnantibus, hostēs fūgērunt (Hostēs fūgērunt quia mīlitēs fortiter pugnābant). 9. Senātus Cicerōnem laudāvit, quod rem pūblicam dēfendisset (dēfenderet). 10. Populus hāc victōriā gavīsus est. 11. Conjūrātōrēs reprehendērunt, quod in cīvium vītās māchinātī essent. 12. Quis mē reprehendat, quod Archiam dēfendam? 13. Lēgātus quod crūdēlis esset reprehēnsus est. 14. Imperātor quod aequus esset laudātus est. 15. Quod vēneris (vēnistī) gaudeō (Tē vēnisse gaudeō). 16. Quod equitēs erant celerēs et fortēs, (hī) captī sunt. 17. Quae cum ita sint, in tabulās hūjus municipiī Archiam ascrībāmus. 18. Propter perīculum domum (domōs) rediērunt. 19. Nāvibus corruptīs in Britanniā mānsit. 20. Quibus parātīs, proficīscāmur. 21. (Vir) Fortis cum sīs, tē nōn repudiābō. 22. Eum quod Archiam nōn laudāret (laudāsset)

---

¹ *Domum* would mean "home," v. g., to Rome, not "to our homes."

reprehendit. 23. Quis Cicerōnem reprehendat, quod haec dīcat?
24. Quae cum ita sint, num audēs negāre tē ad Cicerōnem illō diē
vēnisse?

Exercise 16.—1. Alexander ille tōtum ferē terrārum orbem subēgit
(vīcit). 2. Optimus quisque virtūtem amat. 3. Optimus quisque
amīcitiam laudāvit. 4. Imperātōrem quod deesset reprehendit. 5. Hī sē
ipsōs laudant. 6. Cicerō ille (Praeclārus ille Cicerō) hanc ōrātiōnem
habuit. 7. Sulla, crēdō, illum cīvitāte nōn dōnāvisset. 8. Neque, crēdō,
laudandī sunt Washington et Lincoln! 9. Summum ingenium in eō erat.
10. Negāvit sē hōc negātūrum esse. 11. Sē propter metum Cicerōnis
dēdidērunt. 12. Archiam illum Cicerō dēfendit. 13. Summō ingeniō
praeditus erat. 14. Cicerō Archiam propter suum ergā (in) eum amōrem dēfendit. 15. Cum domicilium Rōmae jam diū habēret, professus
est apud praetōrem (Professus est apud praetōrem, quia jam diū
Rōmae domicilium habēbat).

Exercise 17.—1. Scīmus complūrēs sē nunc ad studium quod religiōnem Chrīstiānam dēlectat atque alit nunc vehementius (ardentius)
cōnferre. 2. Ad ūnum omnēs Parisiī ad summum furōrem pervēnērunt.
3. Quid faciat De Launay? Nihil aliud facere potuit nisi id quod sē
factūrum esse dīxit. Illud tamen facere nōn potuit. 4. Missī sumus ā
rēge ad grātiās tibi agendās (ut tibi grātiās agerēmus). 5. Exposuit
(dīxit) jūdicibus accūsātor, (hōrum) duōrum testium testimōniō, ūnā
cum scrīptīs ab iīs repertīs, quae (in jūdicium) prōlātūrus esset, mani-
festum fore, captīvō (reō)[1] trāditās esse (fuisse) tabulās, in quibus
quae quōque locō terrā marīque rēgiae cōpiae dispositae (distribūtae)
essent ostenderētur, ab eōque hostem dē hīs rēbus (hārum rērum)
saepius certiōrem esse factum. 6. Prīmō (initiō) eīs dīxerat, labōribus
perīculīsque glōriam esse cōnsequendam.

LESSON 4

Exercise 18.—1. Had I not convinced myself of this, I should not
have acted so (Gr. 583). 2. If entertainment were the only object
sought in these pursuits, you would still consider this (form of) mental
occupation most humane (worthy of man) (Gr. 583). 3. If you deny
it, I shall prove it (Gr. 581). 4. If Italy is laid waste, who will praise
you? (Gr. 581). 5. If anyone thinks so (believes this), he is decidedly
in the wrong (badly mistaken) (Gr. 581). 6. If we have been saved,

---

[1] *captīvō* = prisoner of war; *reō* = prisoner at the bar.

should we not give thanks to God (Gr. 581)? 7. If I had said this to
this young man, the Senate would have censured me (Gr. 583). 8. If
he were not a citizen, you would think that he ought to be entered
on the records (Gr. 583). 9. If your country should speak thus, ought
she not to obtain her request? (Gr. 582). 10. If my voice (this voice
of mine) has been trained by his precepts (teaching), ought I not to
help and save him especially? (Gr. 581). 11. If you pay attention to
me, I shall surely succeed in convincing you that he is a citizen (Gr.
581). 12. If my parents feared me, I should go somewhere else
(Gr. 582). 13. If genius of such high order deserves the commendation
of heaven, receive under your protection my client, endowed with
most brilliant genius (Gr. 581). 14. Take away with you all your fol-
lowers; if not all, then as many as possible (Gr. 588). 15. If we have
oral evidence, why do you demand documentary evidence? (Gr. 581).
16. If the citizens feared me, I would leave home (Gr. 583). 17. If I
so live as never to fail my friends in their dangers, who will find fault
with me? (Gr. 581; 550). 18. If I had told him this, would he not
have blamed me? (Gr. 583). 19. If he should come (Were he to
come), what would you do? (Gr. 582). 20. If he were dying, he would
certainly tell the truth (Gr. 583).

Exercise 19.—1. In so wide a range of topics . . . (In so great a
variety of subjects . . .; In the midst of (In spite of) such a variety
of circumstances . . .). 2. To manifest to the eyes of all . . . (To
bring forth into the light of day . . .; To expose to the public
gaze . . .). 3. Such as I possess. . . . 4. By the precepts of many
masters and by wide acquaintance with literature. . . . 5. This is to
be held of little consequence (We must pay little attention to this).
6. Into so many bitter struggles. . . . 7. In the administration of the
state . . . (In the conduct of the government . . .). 8. By an almost
divine quality of (their) natural endowments . . . (By a most excellent endowment of nature itself . . .; In character almost divine . . .). 9. In appreciating and cultivating virtue . . . (To recognize and practice virtue . . .). 10. They add a charm to prosperity
(They enhance success).

Exercise 20.—1. Sī quaerēs (quaesīveris) ā mē, cūr (tantopere) litterīs dēlecter, tibi dīcam. 2. Cūr mē pudeat, sī cōnfiteor mē hīs studiīs
dēlectārī? Sī quī ita sē litterīs (in litterās) abdidērunt, ut suōs tuērī
et servāre nōn possint, eōs pudeat. 4. Sī doctrīnā mentēs excolueritis,
dē magnā rērum varietāte dīcere poteritis. 5. Quis mē reprehendat,
sī ita vīxī, ut numquam amīcōrum perīculīs (difficultātibus) deessem

(dēfuerim)? 6. Quaere argūmenta, sī quae potes. 7. Sī mihi nōn crēditis, clārissimī (amplissimī) quoque et optimī (innocentissimī) virī rēligiōnem habētis. 8. Tabulās sī scīs esse corruptās, cūr (eās) poscis (flagitās)? 9. Sī voluptās mē ab amīcōrum temporibus numquam āvocāvit, cūr mē pudeat? 10. Sī Archiam, ērudītissimum hominem et mihi amīcissimum, dēfendō, quis mē reprehendat? 11. Sī amīcīs dēsim (dēfuerim), tum mē pudeat. 12. Nisi vir bonus fuisset Archiās, Cicerō eum nōn dēfendisset. 13. Nisi Archiās poēta fuisset, hanc ōrātiōnem nōn legerēmus. 14. Nisi Gratius Archiam accūsāvisset, hanc ōrātiōnem nōn habērēmus. 15. Sī litterīs dēlectāris, hanc ōrātiōnem plūrimī facere (aestimāre) dēbēs. 16. Nisi Cicerō multōrum praeceptīs multīsque litterīs cōnfōrmātus esset, hanc ōrātiōnem, quae ā tot virīs summō ingeniō praeditīs laude digna jūdicāta est, numquam scrībere potuisset. 17. Ingenium sine doctrīnā ad glōriam saepe valet. 18. Cicerō nisi vir fortissimus fuisset, numquam sē in tot ac tantōs improbōrum hominum impetūs objēcisset. 19. Mentēs nostrās cōnfōrmēmus intuendīs (illīs) clārissimīs virīs, quōrum virtūtēs litterīs prōditae sunt. 20. Omnēs hae imāginēs in tenebrīs jacērent, nisi litterārum lūmen accēderet (accessisset) (litterīs illustrārentur). 21. Ex hōc fonte (Hinc) exempla virōrum fortium et sapientium hauriō. 22. Nisi litterīs adjūtus esset, numquam (nōn) sē senex ad eās contulisset. 23. Mentēs magnōrum quoque Americānōrum litterīs et studiō cōnfōrmātae sunt. 24. Sī Washington ille (Washington, vir clārissimus) litterās laudāvit, nōnne nōs quoque eās laude dignās exīstimāre dēbēmus? 25. Cicerō, sī Lincoln nōvisset (nōtum habuisset), dīxisset eum nātūrae habitū prope dīvīnō esse praeditum. 26. Nisi Cicerō hanc ōrātiōnem habuisset, numquam nōmen Archiae audīvissēmus. 27. Cicerō, nisi litterīs dēditus fuisset, poētam nōn dēfendisset. 28. Sī Archiās condemnātus (damnātus) esset, Cicerōnem puduisset. 29. Sī Cicerō Catōnem et Fūrium et Laelium nōmināre potuit, nōs quoque possumus nōmināre Washington et Lincoln et Hamilton et Jefferson. 30. Mentēs nostrae, nisi eās excolerēmus, tantam contentiōnem ferre nōn possent. 31. Cicerō contendit (affirmāvit) nātūram sine doctrīnā saepe ad laudem et glōriam valēre posse. 32. Pudeat hōs (hominēs) sī nihil bonī hominibus afferre possunt. 33. Sī Cicerō fassus est sē litterīs esse dēditum, quis jūre eum reprehendat? 34. Rōmae sī fuissēmus, Cicerōnem hanc ōrātiōnem habentem audīvissēmus. 35. Jūdex sī fuissem, Archiam esse cīvem jūdicāvissem. 36. Litterārum studiō penitus (tōtōs) nōs abdere nōn dēbēmus. 37. Sī quī tantum temporis pilae dant (tribuunt), nōnne mihi concēdendum est ut aliquid temporis hīs studiīs tribuam (nōn mihi liceat aliquid temporis hīs studiīs dare)? 38. Sī (ex tē) quaeram (quaesī-verim), cūr hōc librō dēlectēris, quid dīcās? 39. Scrīptōrēs Rōmānī mōrēs multōrum virōrum sapientissimōrum et optimōrum (nōbīs) expressērunt. 30. Quīdam Rōmānī hunc hominem hūmānum in domōs suās recēpērunt.

Exercise 21.—Doctrīnae quidem cōnfōrmātiō magnī dūcenda est. Sī quis tamen ad haec (tālia) studia sē cōnferre nōn potest, fierī potest ut nātūrā et ingeniō ad fāmam et honōrem perveniat. Multī enim sunt, quī sine doctrīnā ad veterum et illūstrium (clārōrum) scrīptōrum et imperātōrum laudem (glōriam) pervēnērunt. Cicerō multōs et clārōs Rōmānōs nōmināre poterat, nōsque multōs et illūstrēs Americānōs ex hōc quoque esse numerō affirmāre possumus. Lincoln enim, quī in plūrimīs perīculīs difficultātibusque populum nostrum servāvit, fuisse ex hōc numerō possumus contendere. Ex hīs quoque erat Alexander Hamilton, qui adulēscentulus, ob ōrātiōnēs (in) quibus nōmen lībertātis celebrāvit, summā laude afficiēbātur (magnōpere laudābātur). Etenim, nātūra sine doctrīnā saepius ad laudem quam doctrīna sine nātūrā valuit. Sed cum ad singulārem et eximiam nātūram accesserit ratiō cōnfōrmātiōque doctrīnae, ad summam ingeniī glōriam pervenītur.

Exercise 22.—1. Quaerēs ā nōbīs, amīce, cūr adeō hīs studiīs dēditī sīmus. 2. Quaerēs ā mē, Cicerō, cūr adeō hōc studiō dēlectēmur. 3. Quaerunt (Quaeritur) ā nōbīs, cūr tam īnfestī (inimīcī) hīs virīs sīmus. 4. Saepe quaerēbātur ā nōbīs Catholicīs cūr iis quī in Novā Hispāniā rēbus praeerant tam īnfestī (inimīcī) essēmus. 5. Quaeris ā mē quae virtus hīs difficillimīs temporibus sit maximē necessāria. 6. Quaeritis ā mē, cūr adeō hunc virum laudēmus. 7. Quaerimus ā vōbīs (abs tē) cūr hoc fēcerītis (fēcerīs).

Exercise 23.—

1. Washington, nisi sibi ā puerō (ā pueritiā) suāsisset,
   nihil esse in vītā magnōpere expetendum,
   nisi lībertātem et exercitium virtūtis,
   numquam prō patriae salūte
   tot ac tantōs (omnēs) cruciātūs (dolōrēs) corporis
   et ipsīus mortis perīculum subīre voluisset.

2. Nam Hannibal, nisi puer constituisset
   populum Rōmānum omnemque honōrem ējus exstinguere,
   numquam, victōriae causā,
   tot ac tanta perīcula atque labōrēs subīsset.

3. Nam Nathan Hale, nisi studiō et praeceptīs multōrum scrīptōrum
   sibi persuāsisset,

nihil esse in vītā exoptandum
nisi virtūtem (probitātem) et aeternam laudem
profectō nōn patriae causā
cruciātūs corporis atque mortem ipsam contempsisset.

LESSON 5

Exercise 24.—1. As soon as Archias grew out of boyhood, he took up the study of writing (Gr. 556). 2. Archias came to Rome, when his reputation had preceded him (Gr. 561). 3. He was at that time acceptable to Metellus (Gr. 920). 4. Archias, after having gone into Sicily in the company of Marcus Lucullus, left that province (Gr. 561). 5. At the time when the law was passed, he had a domicile (home) at Rome (Gr. 560). 6. He made himself known to (registered with) the praetor within sixty days (Gr. 922). 7. This man had now had a home at Rome for many years (Gr. 919). 8. He had a home at Rome for many years before citizenship was granted him (Gr. 924). 9. His inconstancy (unreliability) destroyed all confidence in public documents as long as he was safe (still alive) (Gr. 571). 10. Since the founding of the city many great men have arisen (been born) at Rome (Gr. 932). 11. We ought to admire these things (qualities, achievements) when we see them in others (Gr. 559). 12. Frequently, when he had not written a word (without having written a word), he would declaim offhand (extempore) a large number of excellent verses (Gr. 561). 13. He devoted himself in his old age to the study of writing (Gr. 921). 14. I know what you did the night before (last) (Gr. 920). 15. When Caesar understood (realized, came to know) this, he sent ten cohorts ahead (Gr. 556). 16. That day Manlius was in (under) arms (Gr. 920). 17. He sent soldiers ahead to the hill before the enemy could take it (Gr. 567). 18. Someone or other left while I was pleading the case (Gr. 569). 19. He traveled (marched) for ten hours (Gr. 919). 20. As soon as he saw the enemy, he sent the cavalry against them (Gr. 556). 21. When the enemy saw (had caught sight of) our ships, they left the port (Gr. 561). 22. You were at Rome on that night (Gr. 920). 23. After three days Caesar retired to his camp (Gr. 924). 24. When that was reported, Caesar built (made) a bridge (Gr. 561).

Exercise 25.—1. He was insensible (He was hard-hearted; He was unemotional). 2. The incredible movements of the soul and the agile play of genius . . . (The extraordinary emotions of the heart and the vivacity of genius . . .). 3. He delivers extempore speeches (He speaks on the spur of the moment). 4. His praise rivaled that of the ancient authors (He attained to the fame of the writers of old). 5. It is based on theory, rules, and technique. 6. A poet is inspired by a kind of divine animation (The poet is animated by a sort of praeternatural inspiration). 7. Trained in all that is best . . . (Having enjoyed a first-class education . . .). 8. Besides very many others vie and contend with one another (Very many others too oppose and rival one another).

Exercise 26.—1. Abhinc multōs diēs Rōscius mortuus est (ē vītā excessit). 2. Rōscius quamdiū (dum) vīvēbat, ā Rōmānis laudibus efferēbātur (laudābātur). 3. Nēmō erat, quīn Roscii morte commovērētur (mortem dolēret). 4. Cicerōnem, dum loquēbātur, jūdicēs dīligenter audiēbant. 5. Dīcam, dum concesserītis Archiam esse cīvem. 6. Archiās ut prīmum Rōmam vēnit, summō honōre afficiēbātur. 7. Cum Rōmā dēcessisset (abiisset, exiisset), in Siciliam profectus est. 8. Octāvō post ējus mortem diē, urbs capta est. 9. Quīnque diēbus Rōmam veniēmus. 10. Versūs Archiae lectōs (cum lēgisset), laudāvit. 11. Hāc ōrātiōne ā Cicerōne habitā, jūdicēs Archiam esse cīvem Rōmānum jūdicāvērunt. 12. Cicerōnem Archiam dēfendentem audīvit (Cicerōnem, cum dēfenderet Archiam, audīvit). 13. Homērum, cum mortuus esset (Homērum mortuum), multī cīvem suum vindicābant. 14. Multōs annōs in Italiā est (versātur). 15. Quīnque annīs post (Post quīnque annōs) in Italiam sē contulit (profectus est). 16. Cicerō plūrēs (aliquot) hōrās dīxit (locūtus est). 17. Magnum numerum optimōrum versuum ex tempore dīxit. 18. Simul atque Rōmam vēneris, tēcum loquar. 19. Diē nōnō Archiam ex tempore dīcentem audīvit. 20. Fūgit antequam (Prius fūgit quam) eum in vincula conjicerent.

Exercise 27.—1. Quis tam animō dūrō est, quī (ut) perīculīs (quīn perīculīs) et bellīs quae nunc in orbe terrārum vidēmus nōn commoveātur? 2. Recentī ējus morte nōn commovear? 3. (Ea) Quae accūrātē cogitātēque scrīpsit sī lēgissēs, magnī dūxissēs (aestimāvissēs). 4. Catholicus, cum prō fidē dīmicat (prō fidē dīmicāns), nōnne corporis cruciātūs parvī dūcere dēbet? 5. Cicerō Archiam laudāvit, quod ex tempore versūs dīcere poterat (posset). 6. Quis mē reprehendat, quod versūs Archiae admīrer? 7. Quae (Quās rēs) sī ipsī sēnsū nostrō gustāre nōn possēmus, in aliīs tamen ea (eās) mīrārī dēbērēmus (dēbēbāmus). 8. Hūmānissimus quisque populus poētās admīrātus est. 9. Cicerō negāvit quemquam nōmen poētae umquam violāsse.

Exercise 28.—1. Quis nostrum tam animō dūrō atque agrestī fuit, ut hīs calamitātibus nōn commovērētur? 2. Quis nostrum tam animō agrestī ac dūrō est, ut clārōrum virōrum exemplīs (exemplō) nōn commoveātur? 3. Quis nostrum tam animō agrestī ac dūrō est, ut animus (ējus) Sānctī Aloysiī exemplō nōn commoveātur? 4. Quis nostrum tam animō agrestī ac dūrō est, ut mātris vel patris morte nōn commoveātur? 5. Quis nostrum animō tam dūrō, ut honōrem suum nōn dīligeret? 6. Quis nostrum tam animō dūrō est, ut (corporis) cruciātibus līberīs (in līberōs) illātīs, nōn commoveātur[1] (ut nōn commoveātur, sī (corporis) cruciātus filiīs suīs īnferantur)?

Exercise 29.—1. Sit igitur, jūdicēs, sānctum apud vōs, hominēs rēligiōsissimōs (rēligiōnī dēditōs), hoc Chrīstiānī nōmen. 2. Sit, igitur, jūdicēs, sānctum apud vōs hoc Deī nōmen, quod omnēs gentēs (populī) laudibus extulērunt (laudāvērunt). 3. Sit igitur, cīvēs, sāncta apud vōs haec lēx divīna, quam nūllī umquam barbarī omnīnō condemnāvērunt (repudiāvērunt) (quam nūlla unquam barbara gēns omnīnō condemnāvit). 4. Sit igitur, virī, sānctum apud vōs hoc sacerdōtis nōmen, quod adhūc ā nūllīs umquam barbarīs violātum est (quod nē ā maximē quidem barbarā gente adhuc violātum est).

Exercise 30.—Poētās omnēs populī laudibus extulērunt, nam sānctum semper fuit nōn sōlum in urbibus et apud hūmānissimōs hominēs, sed in silvīs etiam et apud barbarōs poētae nōmen. Neque enim quisquam est (Nēmō enim est) quīn crēdat, poētās quasi quōdam divīnō spīritū īnflarī, eōsque nōn tantum arte et praeceptīs, sed quasi deōrum dōnō (dīs adjuvantibus) versūs scrībere (facere). Apud nōs quoque, nōnne sānctum habendum est (habērī dēbet) hoc nōmen, quod ā nūllō unquam (numquam ā quōquam) violātum est? Nōnne nōs, hominēs rēbus optimīs īnstitūtī, poētās dēfendere et celebrāre (colere) dēbēmus? Graecī suum illum Homērum laudāvērunt; Rōmānī Ennium; cui numerō (ad quem numerum) nōnne Shakespeare, Milton, Thompson, Hopkins, aliōsque multōs adjungāmus (addāmus)?

LESSON 6

Exercise 31.—1. Hoc eum ad percipiendam (cōnsequendam) virtūtem adjūvit. 2. Sē contulit, inquit Cicerō, ad rēs gestās populī Rōmānī celebrandās. 3. Rogāvērunt quis esset nuntius. 4. Quanta esset īnsula nescīvit. 5. Rogāvit unde ortī essent. 6. Post urbem captam (Urbe

---

[1] Cf. Gr. 550.

captā), ad castra rediērunt. 7. Cicerō dīxit Archiam cīvitāte dignum esse quod omne ingenium contulisset ad populī Rōmānī glōriam cele-brandam. 8. Caesar post victōs Gallōs (Victīs Gallīs; Postquam Gallia victa est) in Italiā pugnāre est coāctus. 9. Mīsit nuntiōs quī cognōs-cerent (discerent), quid hostēs poscerent (postulārent). 10. Ponte solvendō (rumpendō) impedīvit (prohibuit) hostēs quōminus (nē) flūmen trānsīrent. 11. Nūllum erat dubium (dubitārī nōn poterat), quīn Archiās esset cīvis. 12. Quis est quī dubitet (Quis dubitet; Ecquis dubitet), quīn Cicerō vir magnus fuerit? 13. Hōc homine repudiandō grātiam (amōrem) sibi omnium ōrdinum conciliāvit. 14. Fortiter pug-nāre fortis mīlitis est. 15. Mē meaque adversus (contrā) inimīcōs dē-fendere vestrum est. 16. Castra esse capta imperātōrī nuntiātum est. 17. Huic quaerentī (Hīs quaerentibus; Interrogātus) respondit, nēmi-nem dubitāre quīn esset ventūrus. 18. Ad virtūtem colendam sē con-tulit. 19. Multum temporis (tempus) rēbus suīs administrandīs tribuit. 20. Classe hostium destruendā vīcimus. 21. Cum eō īre noluērunt (Recūsābant quōminus cum eō īrent). 22. Quis dubitat (dubitet), quīn Cicerō litterās plūrimī dūxerit? 23. Ad urbem incendendam (Incen-dendae urbis) occāsiō erat (fuit) optima. 24. Dīxit eīs hōram ad Cicerōnem interficiendum adesse (vēnisse). 25. Legendō et studendō, inquit, artēs et disciplīnās percipiēmus. 26. Parcendō (ipsīs) hōrum (hominum) amōrem et benevolentiam (tibi) conciliāre potes. 27. Ubi hostēs essent nescīvit. 28. Eum quōminus (nē) urbem ingriderētur impedīvērunt (ingredī prohibuērunt). 29. Quis dubitat (dubitet), quīn litterīs studēre (operam dare) dēbeāmus? 30. Aliōs pudeat, sī numquam tempus tribuērunt, ut amīcōs adjuvārent (ad amīcōs ad-juvandōs). 31. Nescīvī quanta esset pecūnia (quantum pecūniae esset). 32. Quō cōpiae nostrae profectūrae sint rogābunt. 33. Nōlī dubitāre, quīn ventūrus sim. 34. Omnīnō nescio quis sit. 35. Quis dubitāre potest (dubitet), quīn mājor glōriae frūctus possit ex Graecīs versibus percipī quam ex Latīnīs? 36. Quis dubitat (dubitet), quīn victūrī sīmus? 37. Quem nisi Homērus laudāvisset (Nam nisi Homērus eum laudāsset), etiam nōmen ējus quis nunc scīret? 38. Haec, inquit, optima est occāsiō ad Gallōs vincendōs (Gallōrum vincendōrum occāsiō est). 39. Classe aedificandā (classe aedificatā) fūgit (effūgit). 40. Rēs eae quās gessimus (Gesta nostra) orbis terrārum regiōnibus dēfīniuntur (fīnibus continentur). 41. Hoc certē maximum est incitāmentum ad subeunda perīcula et ferendōs labōrēs, ad virtūtem cōnsequendam, ad pugnandum prō lībertāte et vēritāte. 42. Multōs annōs in rēbus gestīs Rōmānōrum scrībendīs (histōriā Rōmānōrum scrībendā) cōnsūmpsit.

43. Saepe accidit ut imperātor dē suīs rēbus scrībī cupiat et aurēs suās etiam poetīs peregrīnīs det. 44. Nostrī illī fortēs virī, sed rusticī ac incultī mīlitēs, sē quoque ducis laudis participēs esse exīstimāvērunt. 45. Quod dē cīvitāte quaeris, quisquis (sī quis) cīvitātī foederātae ascrīptus est, in Italiā domicilium habuit, apud praetōrem Rōmae professus est, cīvis Rōmānus est. 46. Minimē dubitārī potest (Nūllum dubium est; Nōn potest dubitārī) quīn sīmus victūrī. 47. Cicerō Archiam laudāvit quod glōriam populī Rōmānī celebrāvisset. 48. Nē minimum quidem dubium est (Nūllum dubium est), quīn Archiās cīvis sit. 49. Nescīvit (nesciēbat) ubi (mīlitēs) nostrī dispōnerentur (dispositī essent). 50. Legere melius est quam loquī.

Exercise 32.—Model: For, if anyone thinks that less glory comes from the study of Greek poetry, than from that of Latin, he is greatly in error.

1. Nam sī quis minōrem frūctum putat ex studiō linguae Latīnae percipī quam (ex studiō linguae) Gallicae, vehementer errat. 2. Nam sī quis minōrem glōriam putat ex litterīs (studiō litterārum) proficīscī (percipī) quam ex bellō (studiō bellī), vehementer errat. 3. Nam sī quis ad commūnem hominum frūctum putat Rōmānōs minus attulisse (minus hominibus prōfuisse) quam Graecōs, plānē errat (Sī quis putat Rōmānōs minus ad commūnem hominum ūtilitātem attulisse quam Graecōs, plānē errat). 4. Sī quis putat hōs hominēs rērum gestārum suārum (factōrum suōrum) pudēre, vehementer errat. 5. Nam sī quis ējusmodī (tālēs) hominēs sibi persuāsisse putat, nihil esse in hāc vītā (magnōpere) expetendum nisi honōrem (honestātem), plānē errat. 6. Sī quis ad commūnem frūctum putat sānctōs nihil attulisse, vehementer errat. 7. Sī quis (quisquis) minōrem glōriae frūctum putat ex litterīs percipī quam ex reī pūblicae studiō, vehementer errat.

Exercise 34.—Sī cui vestrum mīrum vidētur, optimum quemque litterārum studiō maximē semper dēditum fuisse, Cicerō, ut opīnor, perficiet ut videātis, ex hōc studiō virtūtem et scrībendī bene et dīcendī crēscere (proficīscī, prodīre). Nam in ipsō Cicerōne erat ea dīcendī virtūs, quā amīcōs potuit (posset) adjuvāre, eōsque ex gravissimīs perīculīs et pūblicīs et prīvātīs ēripere (servāre). Contendō quidem (Quīn etiam (imō vērō) affirmō (contendō)), illīs (quidem) temporibus fuisse nēminem quī melius Cicerōne amīcōs dēfendere posset. Nam in eō nōn sōlum summa erat auctōritās—populī enim Rōmānī fuerat cōnsul, eumque ex perīculīs conjūrātiōnis Catilīnae servāverat—sed etiam virtūs in scrībendō et cōpia, quā cēterīs ōrātōribus antecellēbat (quā cēterōs ōrātōrēs superābat, praecēdēbat).

(At) Dīcet (dīcat; dīxerit) aliquis, "(Ut) Fuerit Cicerō ōrātor summus; num hoc probat litterās magnī esse dūcendās (aestimandās; habendās)?" Ipse Cicerō dīcit omnēs artēs, quae ad hūmānitātem pertineant (pertinent), inter sē continērī. Sī quis igitur magnus (praeclārus) vel scrīptor vel ōrātor fierī vult, ad optimārum artium studium sē cōnferre (cōnferat) necesse est. Ex quō studiō et cōnfōrmātiōne doctrīnae nōn modo dīcendī ratiō, sed etiam cōpia et virtūs in scrībendō proficīscētur (proficīscentur).

LESSON 7

Exercise 35.—1. Negant quemquam nisi sānctum honōrem et laudem omnīnō contemnere. 2. Cicerō rogāvit, quis sē reprehenderet, quod litterās laudāret. 3. Dīxit sē nōn sōlum honōris (laudis), sed etiam patriae amōre mōtum (concitātum) esse. Quem sē nōn laudāvisse, quod Catilīnam in exilium ēgisset? Num igitur sē reprehenderent quod id (ita) fēcisset? 4. Rogāvit, quot putārent Archiam esse honōre dignum? Cēterī meminissent, Archiam nōmen populī Rōmānī laude dignum semper dūxisse. 5. Negāsne Archiam magnum poētam fuisse? 6. Dīxit sē, cum Rōmam vēnisset, mē vīsūrum esse. 7. Dīxērunt sē eōs laudātūrōs esse quī sē laudāvissent. 8. Cicerōnis amīcī negāvērunt eum ita ēgisse. 9. Cicerō dīxit ipsōs philosophōs velle praedicārī dē sē; in eīs ipsīs librīs in quibus laudem et honōrem contemnerent (dēspicerent) (eōs) nōmen suum īnscrībere. Num quis dīceret (Num quemquam dīctūrum esse) eōs sibi cōnstāre? 10. Amīcī ingenium ējus probābant. 11. Cicerō dīxit sē jūdicibus sē (ipsum) indicātūrum esse dē quōdam ācrī amōre glōriae, quō libentius Archiae, quod suum (ipsōrum) nōmen populumque celebrāsset, grātiās agerent.

Exercise 36.—1. Dīcō Archiam cīvitātem impetrāvisse, quod Hēracliēnsēs eum dignum putārent. 2. Dīcō eum summō honōre affectum esse, quod amīcus Lūcullōrum esset. 3. Dīcō eum cīvitātem impetrāvisse, quod diū in Italiā habēret domicilium. 4. Dīcō Cicerōnem eum laudāvisse, quod poēta et ērudītus esset. 5. Dīcō cīvitātem esse (fuisse) datam, quod Rōmae domicilium habuisset, Hēracleae ascrīptus esset (fuisset), apud praetōrem professus esset (fuisset). 6. Dīcō lēgātōs Hēracleā vēnisse, quod Lūcullī cupīvissent. 7. Dīcō Cicerōnem negāsse sē posse tabulās pūblicās prōferre quod incēnsae essent. 8. Dīcō, cum amplissimī virī fidem habeāmus, certē rīdiculum (stultum) esse pūblicās tabulās flāgitāre. 9. Dīcō mē gaudēre quod Cicerō Archiam dēfenderit (Cicerōnem dēfendisse Archiam) quia Archiās cīvitāte dignus fuerit. 10. Dīcō optimum quemque poētās admīrārī, quod summō ingeniō (summā ingenī glōriā) praeditī sint. **Exercise 37.**—11. Dīxit eōs tunc guadēre illā victōriā (quod vīcissent; sē vīcisse). 12. Dīxit Cicerōnem, incēnsō tabulāriō (cum incēnsum esset tabulārium; quod incēnsum esset tabulārium; propter tabulārium incēnsum), nōn potuisse tabulās pūblicās prōferre. 13. Dīxit eōs prae timōre nōn potuisse loquī. 14. Dīxit Archiam in cīvitātem ascrīptum esse. 15. Dīxit Cicerōnem propter suum (ipsīus) amōrem (studium) litterārum laudāvisse Archiam.

GENERAL REVIEW EXERCISES

Exercise 38.—1. Argūmenta, sī quae (qua) habēs, expōne. 2. Nē quis mīrētur, dīcam vōbīs, cūr tantopere litterīs dēlecter. 3. Optimus quisque litterās amat (amōre litterārum dūcitur; litterīs dēlectātur). 4. Quispiam dīxit Cicerōnem summum quoque poētam fuisse. 5. Summa in eō erat virtūs (cōnstantia, fortitūdō). 6. Quis nōs reprehendat, quod Cicerōnem laudēmus? 7. Negāvit quemquam hoc concessūrum esse. 8. Fatendum est ūnumquemque nostrum multum tempus (temporis) in legendō cōnsūmere (multum tempus legendō tribuere). 9. Fortissimus quisque mortem timet. 10. Aliī, crēdō, nihil temporis umquam (nūllum unquam tempus) voluptātibus tribuunt. 11. Sī quis putat litterās esse parvī dūcendās, summōrum virōrum, quī sē ad haec studia contulerint, meminerit. 12. Virtūs ēgregia esse dēbet in duce. 13. Archiās ille (vir praeclārissimus) Cicerōnis mentem et animum praeceptīs et doctrīnā suā cōnfōrmāverat. 14. Cicerō dīxit sē Archiae dēditum esse, quod et virtūtem ējus et cōpiam in scrībendō mīrārētur. 15. Gaudeō quod tē ad celebrandam patriam contulistī (Gaudeō tē ad celebrandam patriam tē contulisse).

Exercise 39.—1. Quaeret quispiam: "Nōnne tē pudet tantum temporis (tempus) hīs studiīs tribuere?" 2. Crēdō (Putō) optimum quemque, cūjus laudēs litterīs prōditae sint, excultum esse eā doctrīnā quam Cicerō et Archiās putāverint excellentem et aestimātiōne dignam (Putō omnēs summōs virōs, quōrum laudēs litterīs prōditae sint (sunt), eā doctrīnā ērudītōs (cōnfōrmātōs) esse quam et Cicerō et Archiās optimam et utilem habuerint (habērent, dūcēbant). 3. Dīcunt multōs summōs virōs fāmam (laudem) sine doctrīnā esse assecūtōs. 4. Sunt quī negent haec studia ad virtūtem percipiendam adjuvāre. 5. Cicerō dīxit (dīcēbat) sē mentem (suam) cogitātiōne hominum excellentium cōnfōrmāvisse. 6. Āfricānus, vir fortissimus, ab omnibus Rōmānīs colēbātur, quod, hostibus populī Rōmānī victīs, nōmen commūne magnōpere ornāvisset. 7. Sī quis putat, sōlōs Rōmānōs potuisse nōmināre magnōs virōs, quī sine doctrīnā fāmam assecūtī essent, nostrum illum Lincoln (in memoriam) revocet. 8. Cicerō dīxit studium litterārum domī dēlectāre. 9. Deus sōlus potest (in) rēbus adversīs perfugium nōbīs praebēre. 10. Optimus quisque amat laudatque Deum. 11. Cicerōnem respondentem (Cicerōnis respōnsum) nōn audīvit. 12. Sī quis putat mentem hīs studiīs optimē nōn exercērī, vehementer errat. 13. Num dīcēs ūlla studia senectūtem posse oblectāre? 14. Summa in eō erat auctōritās, quia cōnsul populī Rōmānī fuerat et victōriīs suīs (victīs hostibus; vincendīs hostibus) nōmen Rōmānum celebrāverat. 15. Haec studia, crēdō, ad doctrīnam et glōriam percipiendam nōs nōn adjuvant.

Exercise 40.—1. Ubi Homērus nātus sit nescīmus. 2. Nōs, crēdō, (hominēs) rēbus optimīs īnstitūtī, poētās neque mīrārī neque laudāre dēbēmus. 3. Sī quis vestrum posset (possit) ex tempore dīcere (ōrātiōnēs habēre), eum laudārem (laudem). 4. Post urbem conditam (Ab urbe conditā) ōrātor similis Cicerōnis nōn fuit. 5. Neque est quisquam, quī Archiam nōn laudāret, sī eum ex tempore dīcentem (dīcere) versūs audīvisset. 6. Quantus vir esset vidēre poterāmus. 7. Dīxit neque doctrīnā neque praeceptīs, sed nātūrā ipsā et quōdam deōrum dōnō poētam valēre. 8. In ponte aedificandō (faciendō; Pontem facientēs; Dum pontem faciunt) duo virī interfectī sunt. 9. Nē quis mīrētur Ennium hoc dīcere (hoc Ennī dictum; hoc dīcī ab Enniō)—nōn exercitātiōne aut doctrīnā (disciplīnā), sed habitū prope dīvīnō poēta valet. 10. Num quis igitur reprehendat Ennium, quod poētās ita laudāverit? 11. Mē petentem (poscentem, flagitantem) repudiāvit. 12. Post castellum (praesidium) captum, nōn fuit pugna (nūlla facta est pugna; pugnātum nōn est). 13. Dīcunt plūrimōs dē hāc rē inter sē contendere. 14. Catilīnam mortuum esse (Catilīnae mors) quīnque diēbus nuntiābitur. 15. Haec locūtus est: neminem umquam poētae nōmen parvī dūxisse. Apud populōs maximē barbarōs poētās semper in honōre fuisse. Ipsōs igitur, virī humānissimī cum essent, illud nōmen in honōre habēre dēbēre.

Exercise 41.—1. Cicerō dīcit aliōs (ob id) sōlum laudāre Homērum quod poēta fuerit. 2. Lēgibus et voluntāte suā noster est. 3. Neque quisquam Māriō magis āversus ab hīs studiīs umquam fuit. 4. Nisi Cicerō hanc ōrātiōnem habuisset, ipsum Archiae nōmen ignōtum esset. 5. Sī quaeram abs tē, num litterīs sīs dēditus, quid dīcās? 6. Philosophī sē ipsī (ipsōs) laudant. 7. Adjuvābisne nōs ad moenia aedificanda (munītiōnēs aedificandās)? 8. Cicerō narrat Ennium Āfricānō illī fuisse amīcissimum (carissimum, valde familiārem; familiārissimum Āfricānī illīus). 9. Mīsit quī pontem aedificārent (facerent). 10. Expressit quemadmodum (quōmodo) Pontus captus esset (rēgnum Pontī captum esset). 11. Cicerō dīxit nōmen Rōmānum clārum esse, quod imperātōrēs Rōmānī rēs tantās (tanta) gessissent. 12. Lūcullus, vir fortissimus, paulō ante hanc ōrātiōnem habitam (paulō ante (prius) quam haec ōrātiō habita erat) Pontum vīcit. 13. Classis incēnsa tertiā (diēī) hōrā nuntiāta est (Classem esse incēnsam tertiā diēī hōrā nuntiātum est). 14. Sociōs nostrōs ab interitū servāvit. 15. Fortissimus quisque dux laudem (glōriam; fāmam) cupit et quaerit.

Exercise 42.—1. Legimus Alexandrum illum sēcum habuisse multōs scrīptōrēs, quī rēs suās scrīberent et nōmen (suum) celebrārent (laudārent). 2. Alexander Achillem fortūnātum dūcēbat, quī tam illūstrem scrīptōrem rērum et virtūtum suārum invēnisset. 3. Nisi Homērus vīxisset, multa nōmina nōbīs essent ignōta. 4. Doctissimus quisque Cicerōnem laudat. 5. Sulla, crēdō, eum cīvitāte nōn dōnāvisset. 6. In eō erat scrībendī (in scrībendō) cōpia insignis. 7. Cicerō quaerentī mihi hīs verbīs respondit. 8. Sī quis minus Graecīs litterīs dēlectātur quam Latīnīs, nōn est (optimārum rērum studiō) bene ērudītus. 9. Nōn bene intellēxit, quid hostēs cōgitārent (in animō habērent; mōlīrentur). 10. Negat sē errāvisse (errāsse). 11. Sē ventūrōs esse cum Cicerō Rōmam redīsset pollicitī sunt (prōmīsērunt). 12. Cum esset (Dum erat) Lūcullus (ille), vir clārissimus, in Āsiā, Archiās cum eō erat. 13. Dum Cicerō loquitur, aliquis exiit. 14. Nē pessimus quidem quisque est omnīnō malus et perditus. 15. (Tum) Aderam cum haec ōrātiō habēbātur (Huic ōrātiōnī interfuī). 16. Usque eō laudārī ac nōminārī cupiēbat, ut etiam poētīs in prōvinciīs nātīs, dummodo dē rēbus suīs (gestīs) scrīberent, praemium tribueret. 17. Duābus hōrīs Rōmam vidēbimus.

Exercise 43.—1. Nōn dubitō quīn Cicerō vēra dīxerit. 2. Omnem vim suam ad Lūcullōs celebrandōs cōnferre nōn dubitāvit. 3. Quis dubitat quīn Cicerō commemorātiōnem nōminis suī cum omnī posteritāte adaequāverit? 4. Optimus quisque labōribus et cūrīs sē frangit. 5. Multī populī de vītā et lībertāte dīmicant (certant). 6. Post rem pūblicam cōnstitūtam populus Americānus in multīs perīculīs labōribusque versābātur. 7. Cōgitātiōnēs nostrae regiōnibus (fīnibus) hūjus mundī nōn terminantur (sunt circumscrīptae). 8. Sānctī, nisi Deum sibi (ante oculōs) semper prōposuissent, num sē tot labōribus frēgissent? 9. Etiam post tot annōs Cicerō summīs laudibus effertur (in honōre habētur). 10. Lēgātōs occīsōs esse secundā diēī hōrā nuntiātum est. 11. Vīta sine litterīs est mors.

Exercise 44.—1. Post Rōmam conditam. . . . 2. Rōmā conditā . . . (Cum Rōma condita esset . . .; Postquam Rōma condita est). 3. Post pontem aedificātum . . . (Ponte factō). 4. Ab urbe conditā. . . . 5. Cum pōns aedificatus esset . . . (Ponte aedificātō . . .; Postquam (ut) pōns aedificātus est . . .). 6. Ā Rōmā conditā . . . (Post Rōmam conditam . . .). 7. Optimārum (līberālium) artium studiō. . . . 8. Multīs litterīs legendīs. . . . 9. Multīs litterīs legendīs. . . . 10. Studium scrībendī. . . . 11. Studium litterārum. . . . 12. Pudeat eōs. . . . 13. Pudeat eōs. . . . 14. Pudeat eōs. . . . 15. Cūr mē pudeat? 16. Quis mē reprehendat? 17. Quis mē reprehendat? 18. In rē pūblicā administrandā . . . (In rēbus pūblicīs administrandīs . . .).

Exercise 45.—1. Ab urbe conditā nōn fuit tantus ōrātor quantus Cicerō. 2. Cūr mē pudeat, sī mē ad scrībendī studium cōnferō? 3. Quis mē reprehendat, sī mē ad litterārum studium cōnferō? 4. Et doctrīna et nātūra ad mōrēs excolendōs adjuvant. 5. Multīs litterīs (legendīs) ad fāmam et glōriam parvī dūcendam (parvī faciendam, neglegendam) adductus est (Multīs litterīs (legendīs) fāmam et glōriam parvī dūcere didicit). 6. Post Rōmam conditam (Ā Rōmā conditā) nēmō ad optimārum artium studium dīligentius sē contulit. 7. Ad ea omnia studia ex quibus dīcendī virtūs dūcitur (crēscit) dīligenter sē contulit. 8. Quis mē reprehendat, sī negō post Rōmam conditam quemquam dīligentius Cicerōne ad litterārum studium sē contulisse? 9. Eōs pudeat quī litterīs studēre (operam dare) nōlunt, quia somnō et voluptāte āvocantur (āvertuntur).

Exercise 46.—Archiās Graecus erat, quī Antiochīā Rōmam vēnerat, cum Cicerō esset quīnque annōs nātus (puer quīnque annōrum) et mōre (cōnsuētūdine) illōrum temporum apud Lūcullum, ūnum ex prīncipibus virīs Rōmae, habitābat; cūjus poētae fāma in sōlā (eā) ōrātiōne cōnsistit (ex sōlā (eā) ōrātiōne pendet), quam Cicerō prō hōc vetere magistrō suō et amīcō posteā habuit. Nam quamquam versūs (poēmata, carmina) illum ad celebrandōs virōs illūstrēs Rōmānōs scrīpsisse (fēcisse) scīmus, nē ūnus quidem ē versibus ējus servātus est.

Exercise 47.—Catilīna, urbe relictā (postquam ex urbe excessit; cum ex urbe exiisset) cum Mānliō (quī erat) in Etrūriā sē conjūnxit, et cum conjūrātōs Rōmae captōs et morte esse multātōs (interfectōs esse) comperīsset (audīvisset, accēpisset), cum hominum seditiōsōrum (impiōrum) nōn minus vīgintī mīlibus in Galliam iter facere parābat. Sed Quīntus Metellus, quī cum exercitū satis magnō in agrō Picēnō